# How is my TEDDY?

Leron Young

Copyright © 2015 Leron Young
All rights reserved.

ISBN: 1502408562
ISBN 13: 9781502408563
Copyright Number: **TXu 1-935-866**

# INTRODUCTION

The acronym TEDDY has improved my life, and is continuing to improve it. Once you are able to implement some of these changes, your life will improve, and you want have the desire to return to your old ways of doing things. The acronym TEDDY is easy to remember. It's a word we can relate to, as it's a very common name in the United States. *T* stands for Thinking, *E* stands for Eating and Exercising, the first *D* stands for Drinking, the second *D* stands for Doing, and *Y* represents You.

Like most people today, I've had my share of challenges—and continue to have them. The difference now is that I have a different mind-set to handle them. I have a tool now to check myself when I get off my path. I have the acronym TEDDY.

If I'd known twenty to thirty years ago what I know now, I would've made some different choices. But that's OK, because I've learned some valuable things about myself through those experiences. I didn't know the importance of monitoring what I was thinking and what I was feeling. I depended on other people to tell me what they thought and how they felt about things.

I didn't understand the power I had within myself, nor did I trust it. I was making things outside myself more real than I should have. I was making things outside myself more important than what was inside me. I was afraid of listening to my own truth.

Now that has changed. TEDDY has helped me make the changes I needed to make. It is a tool that helps me when things seem to not be going well. I say "seem" because it is all about perception.

Many forces outside us are attempting to control us. We need a tool to help us when we find ourselves being manipulated by these forces. We are also influenced greatly by our egos. This can be a real challenge for us, and we need tools to counter some of the images and forces we experience every day.

We have been conditioned as a people to accept anything that is advertised to us. I love this country and all the freedom it has given us. But some of the freedoms it has given us have caused us to have less control of our lives in terms of being healthy and happy. We have not had the knowledge or the discipline to control ourselves against some of the negative influences.

The media has had the freedom to influence our habits and thoughts with its massive use of technology. We have the freedom to eat foods that are very unhealthy for us. We don't realize how unhealthy they are, because no one has told us, and we haven't done the research ourselves. We have the freedom to drink contaminated water and not realize the extent of its damage. Not knowing these things has caused us to be unhealthy and not live the kind of life that brings us joy, happiness, and fulfillment.

The acronym TEDDY is a tool we can make a habit of using when our minds are agitated or confused. We can use TEDDY when our lifestyles are not bringing us the kind of peace and joy we deserve. TEDDY has helped me to stay focused on the important things and stay on the path to fulfillment. We all have the power to make that happen.

    We will always have challenging experiences. It's not what we're going through that matters, but what we are being while going through them. I try to keep a positive attitude during those times that are challenging. Being in control of ourselves and remaining positive does not always come easily. There will be some challenges initially. The outcome usually turn out better in the long run if we remain positive. Our upbringing and conditioning have caused us to create some habits that need to be broken. We have the power to break these habits, and we must break them, if we want to see changes in our lives. We must first break them internally. We were taught to handle our problems or concerns externally and not internally. When we begin to handle them internally, we will see and experience some wonderful changes in our lives.

We now have at our disposal tools that all of us can use to bring us the kind of knowledge we need to change our lives. We have access to more information than we have ever had, thanks to the Internet and social media. People are starting to awaken. We also know that there is a lot of unhealthy information on the Internet. Our hearts will lead us to the right places on the Internet when we listen to them for guidance. "When the student is ready, the teacher will appear." The soft voice that we hear within us is much wiser than we are. We will be guided in unexpected ways. Someone may say something that influences you deeply without the person even knowing it. We may look in a child's eyes and get a great revelation. We may come across a book or an article that speaks to our inner truth. A certain book may suddenly fall off the bookshelf into our hands. It may come from a song we hear on the radio or television. The universal power, or however you identify our creator, will bring you the situation or wisdom you need when it is time.

Now is the time for us to make major changes so we can live the lives we've dreamed of. We have no choice other than to change. Change is going to take place regardless of what we do. We want to change ourselves for the better. Something has been missing, and we haven't had the knowledge to fix it. To say it another way, we've had the knowledge, but it has been buried deep down inside of us, and we didn't know it was there. We didn't know we had the diamonds.

As the dawn of a new day begins to come forth and dispel the darkness, it is time for our awakening.

This information is just a small way for me to contribute to a movement taking place in the world. I have been fortunate enough to find some of the knowledge that has caused me to make major changes in my life. It has caused me to become closer to God, who dwells within us. It has caused me to have a greater awareness of myself. It has caused me to feel closer to humanity and nature. It has caused me to know that I am wonderfully loved and have the capacity to love more wonderfully. I'm not where I want to be, but, thank God, I'm not where I was. What has helped me is what I'm about to share with you on the following pages.

I got the idea for TEDDY while at a conference for a company I work with called Veritas Instrument Rentals. The conference was in Orlando, Florida, in the winter of 2013. I was in my hotel room doing some reading, and the question came to my mind: How is my TEDDY? The acronym just popped into my head.

Before that experience in Orlando, I had been paying more attention to my mind in terms of how I'd been thinking and feeling at any given time. Not just surface thinking, but deep thinking. I had been paying more attention to what I was eating and whether I was getting enough exercise. I have seen people benefit from becoming vegetarian or vegan, or just from changing their eating habits. I have seen the benefits of exercise in their lives. I learned about the benefits of drinking alkaline water. I had been becoming more aware of all the things people could do to improve their lives. What actions could I take to improve my life and the lives of others? What question could I ask myself that would call attention to how I could improve my life? What question could do the same thing for others? The acronym TEDDY came to my mind, and the question, "How is my TEDDY?" was born.

# HOW IS MY THINKING?

The letter "T" in TEDDY stands for the word "thinking." Many of us don't understand the dynamics of thinking. We think that thinking is something our minds just do, and sometimes it doesn't have much significance at all. We think it's just something we do within ourselves, and that no one knows what's going on in our minds.

Thoughts are always going through our minds. It's when we embrace those thoughts and act on them that they take root. They then begin to influence our lives and the lives of others. They influence our lives in ways we can't imagine. We don't realize we're sending signals to the universe through our thoughts and feelings. At some point we will receive those signals back. Those signals will attract experiences and situations that correspond to those frequencies and energies we sent out. Have you ever heard an echo that occurs when someone who is in a cave says the word "hello"?

I was once working in the medical field as an engineering systems specialist. I want to illustrate how manipulating frequencies are used in many universal principles.

I was installing, servicing, and maintaining MRI and CAT scanners in the medical field. MRI is an acronym for magnetic resonance imaging. An MRI takes images of the body using a strong magnetic field and other supporting technologies. CAT is an acronym for computerized axial tomography. It also takes images of the body, using radiation and other supporting technologies.

I'm going to use some of the principles of the MRI to make my point: Our physical body is made up of about 65–70 percent water. Water molecules/protons resonate at different frequencies in our bodies, depending on the environment they are in. The strength of the magnetic field of the MRI that I was working on was 0.5, 1.0, and 1.5 tesla.

When a person is having an MRI, the protons in their bodies are excited by transmitting a radio frequency signal to them that's at the same frequency their protons are spinning/resonating. The protons in the body that are being excited transmit back a signal once the resonant frequency is determined by the MRI's technology. The signal that is captured is then reconstructed into an image that reveals information about the person's anatomy. A signal is transmitted to your body's protons and then a signal is received back from your body's protons, such as in an echo. This is the basic principle of how the MRI works, and it's analogous to our sending our thoughts and feelings out into the universe. It is also analogous to the person saying hello in a cave, as I explained. How an MRI acquires the data is much more complicated, and I don't want to bore you with that at this time. But this principle is also analogous to how our mind and feelings relate to our physical world. Our minds think thoughts at different frequency levels. These thoughts represent certain emotions we have about ourselves. These feelings or emotions are transmitted throughout the universe. They return to us, reflecting the same frequency, energy, or emotions we sent out. They return as physical matter or the conditions of our daily lives. They return as events of love or fear, depending on what we have been feeling and thinking.

Everything in the universe is vibrating at many different frequencies—solids, liquids, gasses, light, sound, X-rays, and thoughts. Everything in life is a combination of these energies or frequencies. Every thought we think, word we speak, and action we take can be identified by a combination of these energies or frequencies.

Since we're discussing thinking, consider the saying, "As a person thinks, so is he/she." That's where he or she is at that time. I do know we're greater than our thoughts, but this is a good place to start this conversation.

What does that saying mean to me? We are all thinking constantly. We think consciously and unconsciously. How we feel and respond to all the situations in our lives is directly related to how we are thinking. Whatever our situation in life is reflects what we are thinking and what others are thinking.

God gave us the power to create by using thoughts, words, and actions. The mind is like a magnet. It attracts to it what it is thinking. If you think fearful thoughts, you will be attracting fear and the conditions associated with fear. If you think about and feel love, you will attract love and the conditions associated with love. Most of the time we are not aware of what we are doing with our minds and how our thinking is affecting us.

We are also affected by the combined thinking of our nation or whatever environment we are in. At our level of development, we don't have any control over the combined thinking of our nation or what ever environment we are in. But we do have control over how the combined thinking of others may affect us. We can make ourselves happy or content no matter what we are experiencing.

I have come to understand that our thoughts are not who we really are, but a starting point for changing our lives. We are much bigger than our thoughts. We must be aware that the ego (Edging God Out) is also using the mind for its agenda. The problem is we don't pay enough attention to our minds and eventually find ourselves in situations and events that are unpleasant, especially when the ego has taken over. We need to be aware of what is controlling our minds. Is it our ego or our heart? Our heart is our higher self or our higher consciousness. We are the unspeakable silence and space used by thought. We are the consciousness that's aware of our thoughts. We shouldn't think we're just the sum of our thoughts. We should just be aware of them.

    Many situations we find ourselves in are the result of negative thoughts. Our words and actions also play a major role, but it all begins with a thought. Get in the habit of thinking about what you're thinking about. When you find yourself being worried, angry, or fearful, pay attention to your thoughts and feelings and how you're reacting to them. Then change them. When you find yourself being envious, sad, or frustrated, again pay attention to your thoughts and your reaction to them. Then change them. It is just that simple. If we pay attention to how we're feeling, it's a good indication to how we are thinking. I'm not saying you won't have some challenges. But even so, you can still experience peace, joy, and a feeling of well-being while going through them. You can become the master of your mind and your experiences. Know that peace and joy may not always be around you, but they will always be within you if you know how and when to access them.

Your true self is the one who is observing the mind's chatter. When you don't pay attention to how these thoughts affect you, your life will be like a roller coaster. Your feelings and emotions will be very unstable, depending on what you're experiencing, especially when those feelings and emotions are fear-based. What you experience will be the result of what you allow your mind to think. You will experience the results of your actions from the so-called past. I read something that stated, "The sins of the past will wash onto the shores of today for a time." It's a cycle. Many circumstances we find ourselves in are the results of fear-based thinking. We need to observe and control our thinking if we want our lives to change.

You may worry that it's boring to watch your every thought day in and day out. At times it is tedious, but trust me, it's better than letting the mind/ego totally run your life. Your mind will eventually get the message and give your heart more authority to create your experiences. Remember, in the Bible Jesus says, "Let not your heart be troubled." Moses, Buddha, Muhammad, and others have also left us great words of wisdom. Jesus's words mean to me that you have to control your mind and heart.

Keep your mind on the thoughts that come from your higher self, the thoughts of joy and gratitude and the feeling of love and abundance. Ask yourself, what is the greatest joy I want to experience while living this life? How can I better serve my family, my country, and humanity with the gifts Almighty God has given me?

Smile more. Laugh more. Let your mind have bigger dreams than you've ever had before. Be thankful and grateful for what you already have. Have a greater perception of yourself. See yourself through the filter and perception of love, and not fear. Always ask yourself throughout the day, "How are my thoughts? How is my TEDDY?"

If your thoughts are fearful or focused on all the emotions that come with fear, just change them. Take your mind away from fear and to feelings of love and actions of love. "Let not your heart not be troubled." You have the power to resist your feelings of anger, jealousy, envy, and loss, and to resist the desire to speak of your harmful thoughts about yourself, your brother, or your sister. You have the power to change your life simply by changing your thoughts. You are not your thoughts. You are the unspeakable silence and space your thoughts use. Your thoughts only become you when you choose them, speak of them, and act on them. You are the *observer* of your thoughts.

I like to use the analogy of a person having a well-fertilized garden ready to be planted. This garden represents the mind. He/she is ready to start planting seeds in the garden. The seeds represent the thoughts he/she will be selecting to plant in the garden. There are two different types of seeds: seeds of fear and seeds of love. The gardener has the choice to select from either of these two. The garden doesn't care which seed is selected. It's going to grow no matter what. That's how it is with our lives. Whatever thoughts we choose are going to be planted in our garden/lives. Whatever comes forth from our garden is what we are going to eat. Whatever thoughts and feelings we send out into the universe with our minds will be manifested as what we are going to experience. Just like an echo. Thoughts of sickness bring about poor health. Thoughts of poverty bring about one experiencing poverty. Thoughts of gratitude, joy, wellness, and love will eventually cause one to experience joy, greater well-being, and love.

I have experienced a lot of setbacks, as all of us have. I have gone through the mill and wondered if things would ever get better. It wasn't until I changed my thinking and feelings about all of my situations that my life started to change. I have learned to be happy and grateful no matter what I'm experiencing at the moment. I must say to you that it hasn't always been easy to change my thinking, because I was in the habit of dwelling on fear more than love. Habits can be difficult to break. It takes time to create them, and it does take time to get rid of them. But believe me, it can be done. I used to smoke cigarettes, marijuana, take pills and do all kinds of unhealthy things to my body. Just by changing my thinking about myself, and loving myself and others, I found the strength to make the changes I needed to make. You can do the same thing. It's only a thought away.

"If there is a wave, there must be an ocean". If there is a you, there must be God. It is wonderful. God is greater than you can imagine and God dwells in you. Think about that.

# HOW IS MY EATING AND EXERCISING?

The next letter in the acronym TEDDY is the letter *E*, for eating. Eating helps us sustain our physical bodies. Eating is something we must do, and it can give us great satisfaction. Almighty God has placed in our midst an abundance of natural foods. We also have in our midst food that has been manipulated and has very little nutritional value. We must come to the realization that food is our medicine—we are what we eat.

We have an obesity epidemic in this country and throughout other parts of the world. There is a statistic that says that 60 percent of the people in this country are overweight and 30 percent are obese. That means only 10 percent of our people are considered physically healthy. I want to make the point that just because you are thin that doesn't make you healthy. Also, because you are a little overweight that doesn't mean you're unhealthy. Some people are just naturally thin or a little heavy. Other factors come into play, such as getting enough exercise to stay fit, which I will talk about later.

When I was younger, I didn't care or pay much attention to what I was putting in my body in terms of food. If it tasted and smelled good, I would eat it. When you are young, your body can tolerate eating unhealthy food better than it can when you're older. I used to eat all I wanted to and didn't pick up any extra weight. Now I am paying much more attention to my weight and what I am eating.

A few years ago, I started having some health issues. I was tired all the time, especially when I tried to walk up stairs. I was also beginning to be overweight. I eventually went to see a doctor. He sent me to the hospital, and they gave me a stress test and monitored me for a day. They didn't find anything, but a doctor wanted to put me on medication for my heart. I decided I didn't want to go on any medication. Guess what the doctor said to me after I told him? "You have to go on something."

Unfortunately, most doctors are trained to put us on some form of medication to solve the health issues we may have. The doctor talked very little about the food I was eating. The emphasis was on giving me medication. I don't want to sound as though I don't appreciate doctors for what they do—attempting to make us well. I do appreciate them and I know that most of them mean well, but I also realize that there are other ways to solve some of our health issues than being put on lots of medications.

I knew not eating right and not getting enough exercise were causing some of my problems. I knew that if I wanted to feel better, I had to do something about it. Had I not made the decision to eat better and get more exercise, my health would have declined further.

A lot of us are sick and don't even realize it. We seem not to be conscious of what we are doing to ourselves. We are not concerned about what we are putting in our bodies. Many in the food industry are not giving us the facts about the products they are selling.

Their food is filled with preservatives, chemicals, saturated fat, sugars, and all types of ingredients that are causing us to be unhealthy. A lot of the food that we eat is calorie rich, but nutrient poor. Look at our children and notice that they are overweight and not getting enough exercise. Something is wrong, and we need to do something about it. That something is paying more attention to what we are putting in our bodies and then making some changes.

Your body is forgiving to an extent. It will allow you to mistreat it, but only for a certain amount of time. Then it will get your attention. It will let you know you've been mistreating it and that now you'd better do something about it. That something is getting a checkup and then paying more attention to what you're eating.

Many of our illnesses such as heart disease, diabetes, strokes and others are caused by poor nutrition. We have so much information right at our fingertips that can help us solve many of our health problems. We just need to know what the information is and where to find it. Then we need to take action. None of us should wait until our conditions become critical. Unfortunately, many of us do. Even then, it's not too late to get back on a healthy eating routine.

Listen to your body. Our bodies will tell us when something is out of balance. It may be very subtle at first. The key is to listen and pay attention. Your body will give you much joy if you are in tune with it. It will also give you much trouble if you don't take care of it. It is the vehicle you use to take you through this life. I like riding in a well-built, fine-tuned vehicle more than I do riding in a broken-down jalopy. We know we must keep our automobiles tuned up if we want them to run well. It's the same for our bodies. And our bodies are much more important than our automobiles.

What is your vehicle like? Have you been taking care of it? When is the last time you had an oil change and tune-up? When is the last time you visited a good doctor and had a physical? When I say a good doctor, I mean one that doesn't want to fill you up with lots of pharmaceuticals for a long time in an attempt to solve preventable health issues.

Are you happy about how you feel and look? Are you giving your body the proper nutrition it needs to stay healthy? If you think about it long enough and observe yourself, the answer will become very clear to you. Have you lost a tremendous amount of energy over the years? We know that getting older does cause some loss of vitality. We know that we don't have the same stamina we had when we were in our youth. But we can slow down the process of getting older by eating properly and taking care of our bodies. It is difficult to be truly happy if we are unhealthy.

Are you still smoking cigarettes, using drugs, or drinking lots of alcohol? If the answer is yes, it should be obvious to you that you need to stop doing those things and pay more attention to what you're eating. Are you aware of the amount of sugar, salt, fat, and artificial ingredients you're putting in your body and how they're affecting you? How do you feel after eating certain foods? Do you feel sluggish, weak, or want to take a nap after eating certain foods? These may be signs that you're not giving your body proper nutrition. When we eat better, we do everything better. I'm not suggesting that you become a vegan or vegetarian. I'm not one myself, but I am working toward being more health conscious when it comes to what I eat. I do know that I feel a lot better after changing my diet. I hope at some point you will do the same thing.

How is your TEDDY today when it comes to eating?

# HOW IS MY EXERCISING?

*E* also represents exercise in TEDDY. Let me first say that exercising should be done regardless if we overindulge in eating. If we decide to overindulge in eating, we must consider exercising to burn off the extra pounds we'll accumulate by overeating. The extra calories must go somewhere. It's hard to ignore the fact that we need to exercise. We just get lazy when it's time to do it.

Most Americans don't have the willpower to exercise. We're not encouraged enough to do so by our nation's health-care system or the media. We are somewhat encouraged, but not to the level that we should be. Overeating, not exercising, and not getting enough rest will cause us to have many problems.

Keeping people unhealthy can be very profitable for the pharmaceutical industry. It became clear to me why there are always pharmaceuticals in most of the major stores where we buy our food. This is where we purchase a lot of the unhealthy food that's making us sick. Pharmaceuticals should also be in all those fast-food chain restaurants. I won't mention their names here, but I'm sure you know which ones I'm talking about. On top of eating unhealthy foods, we're not getting the exercise or rest we need.

I take my hat off to the first lady, Michelle Obama. She and others have attempted to make our nation more health conscious, especially our young people.

The automobile is one of the things that caused and continues to cause us not to get much exercise. It has brought us a lot of comfort and convenience, but it also has taken away a lot of our will to exercise. I've seen people who live only a block or two away from a store get in an automobile and drive there. I know, because I've done it myself. I've seen people one floor above or below their destination in a building take the elevator. I know, because I've done it myself. Let's get more active in everything we do. When you see the opportunity to get more exercise, force yourself to do it, and soon it will become a habit.

Television is another one of the things that continues to cause us to be sedentary. Being a "couch potato" kind of says it all. Look at how much unnecessary television we and our children watch throughout the year. Look at how much time our children spend playing video games, hardly getting any exercise. It's no wonder we have an obesity epidemic.

It is well documented that exercising has many benefits. Being active will improve your overall cholesterol by boosting your HDL (high density lipoprotein), which is your good cholesterol. It also will lower your LDL (triglycerides), which is your bad cholesterol.

Physical exercise will help prevent and manage a wide range of health problems, such as strokes, diabetes, arthritis, and many others. It will also help those who are suffering from depression. There are many benefits from exercising. You don't have to do anything strenuous. Just simply walking will get the job done. I go to a sports and learning center in my neighborhood to work out at least three days a week, sometimes four. It has been wonderful. Being around other people who are exercising helps to keep me motivated. I walk at least two miles three or four times a week. I do a lot of other exercises as well, but just walking is good enough for people who are just starting to exercise.

Did you know that exercise will improve your mood? It will give you an emotional lift, boost your confidence and self-esteem, and improve your appearance. It will boost your energy, improve muscle strength, and improve endurance. Exercising will deliver more oxygen and nutrients to your tissues and help your cardiovascular system work more efficiently. When your heart and lungs work more efficiently, you have more energy as you go throughout the day. Proper breathing is another key factor in exercising. There is a lot of information written about proper breathing. Please do the research. Yoga and other techniques can be very helpful.

I've had the opportunity to travel. I've visited Holland and Ghana. I saw firsthand how people in other cultures benefit from riding bikes and just walking. Neither nation has the obesity epidemic we do here in the United States, at least they didn't at that time. They depend more on their transportation systems, on riding bikes, and on just walking. The benefit of being more active was very obvious in those countries.

How is your TEDDY today when it comes to exercising? Let's find more ways of staying physically active. Let's also be aware that we need plenty of rest after exercise. We will feel and look a lot better.

# HOW IS MY DRINKING?

*D* represents drinking in TEDDY. Drinking water every day is necessary to maintain proper health. Our body is composed of about 65 to 70 percent water. Water is to the body what oil is to an automobile. The automobile will not run without oil. Nor will your body function well without the proper amount of water. Dehydration is a condition that occurs when lost body fluids exceed the amount of body fluids taken in by our bodies. When we lose too much water, our bodies become out of balance and we can become seriously ill, even die.

Please pay attention to your fluid intake, especially water intake. Also pay attention to the color of your urine. If it is deep yellow or amber and has a strong odor, that's a sign you are close to becoming dehydrated. When you have sufficient water in your body, your skin will look radiant. Your urine will become clearer. You also get rid of unwanted toxins in your body when you drink the proper amount of alkaline water. It also causes your body to be less acidic. How do we know if our body is acidic from a lack of drinking alkaline water? I got the following information from a company called Enagic. A Japanese company that produce kangen water using advanced Japanese water technology. The Japanese are some of the healthiest people in the world. Here are some of the conditions they say you could acquire because of your body becoming acidic due to the lack of drinking enough alkaline water:

1. constipation
2. muscle and joint pain
3. rapid or irregular heartbeat
4. heartburn or diarrhea
5. food allergies
6. metallic taste in the mouth
7. cold sores
8. depression
9. asthma

10. migraine headaches

11. insomnia

12. swelling

13. dark circles under the eyes

14. rheumatoid arthritis

15 chronic digestive problems

16. osteoporosis

17. multiple sclerosis

18. heart and circulatory disease

19. diabetes

20. all forms of cancer

These are just some of the conditions that can be the result of our bodies being acidic. Many benefits can be gotten simply by drinking enough water, a proper diet, exercise, and rest.

I learned about the benefits of drinking alkaline water from the same company that produce Kangen water using advanced water technology. The company Enagic does not say that drinking Kangen or alkaline water will cure disease such as cancer. But drinking alkaline water has greatly improved my overall health and well-being along with others. Drinking alkaline water has many benefits. Here are some of them:

1. It flushes the body of toxins and acidic waste.
2. It helps reverse degenerative diseases.
3. It hydrates the body at a cellular level.
4. It strengthens your immune system against diseases.
5. It causes healthy digestion and elimination.
6. It can enhance sleep, give you more energy, and help you lose weight.

There are many more benefits from drinking an optimal amount of alkaline water. I find that the best time is when I first get up in the morning.

At one time I didn't know I wasn't getting the proper amount of water. My body was craving it, but I really didn't feel thirsty. Sometimes we can feel hungry, but our body is really craving more water. Now the more I drink alkaline water, the more I crave it.

I know that all of us don't have access to alkaline water. I purchased the Kangen machine, which makes alkaline water, and I have been giving the water to some family members and friends. I get many testimonies from them about how drinking the water has improved some of their health issues. If you don't have access to alkaline water, at least test the water you're drinking. If the water is acidic, try to get access to better drinking water.

Certain bottled water is very acidic, and we shouldn't drink it if we can help it. Do the research yourself. I tested some of their water myself and I was very surprised how acidic the water was. In fact, my regular tap water tested much less acidic than the bottled water I was buying from that company.

Pay more attention to the water you're drinking. Don't be fooled by the way it looks. It can look clean and refreshing, but still be very acidic. Find out how to have your water tested. It's a very simple process. The bottom line is you must get an optimal amount of nonacidic water to remain healthy.

Are you drinking enough water on a daily basis? Ask yourself, "How is my TEDDY today?"

# HOW IS MY DOING?

The other *D* in TEDDY represents doing. Sometimes we find ourselves just busy, busy, busy and not getting very much accomplished. We often do things out of habit—not what works or what matters. If we became more aware of what our purpose is and set priorities, we will accomplish more and be happier doing so.

We can be pulled in many directions if we're not making the best choices for ourselves. Pay closer attention to that higher calling that has been trying to get your attention. It doesn't call us as loudly as the world does, but it's our true calling. We must pay more attention to it.

We find ourselves doing things that are contrary to what we should be doing and what we are naturally good at doing. We can hear our true purpose calling us when we have a job that is unfulfilling. It calls us when we're seeking to become a medical doctor when we're actually really gifted as an artist.

Often we do things just to make money. Many of us are guilty of that. Ask yourself, are you doing things out of fear, or are you doing things out of love? Are you living a life you can admire? Are you following your bliss?

    Unfortunately, most of us are taught to make decisions that are out of line with who we really are. We may find ourselves working hard at the wrong things. When I say "wrong," I mean not working with our gifts. Let's train and educate ourselves in the fields we're good at, and not just the fields that make a lot of money. Please don't think that I'm against making money, because I'm not. I know how important it is to have the resources we need to survive and to follow our dreams. I also know how important it is to have a sense of well-being in spite of having money. We can have both, and we should. Just be yourself. I came across a saying not long ago. You may not believe it, but I feel that it's true. "In order to have everything, you must want nothing."

One of my guitar students just turned eighty-three. He said learning to play the guitar is something he's always wanted to do. He has chosen to develop something he has a passion for even at this stage of his life. I see the joy he gets when he comes to my class. He may have had the desire to play an instrument as a child, but didn't have access to an instrument then.

Whenever we see any child who has a natural gift, we should try to see that he or she gets the right tools to develop that gift. It is important to cultivate all of our children's talents and gifts. Those talents and gifts will bring much joy to them, and us, eventually. They will be doing things that will benefit the entire world. It's wonderful when people do things that bring joy to the world.

I've seen people who were gifted in art but who chose to work in the field of computer science. I'm not saying that anything is wrong with computer science, because it's a good field. But if that's not what brings you joy at the cellular level, you are in the wrong field, and you need to make a change if you want to be happy. Many of us are not willing to make that change out of fear. We don't think we can make a living at what we are good at, and we stay miserable working at something we don't enjoy. I realize how difficult it can be to make major decisions. Doing so takes a lot of courage, and you may feel some fear in the process. Once you make the decision to go after your dream while using your gift, your life will change for the better.

If you are gifted in computer science or some type of engineering field, don't try to be a full-time artist. I'm not suggesting you shouldn't study other fields of knowledge. It's good to learn as much as you can hold. Study and pursue what brings you joy and fulfillment.

What are you doing with your life now? This should be the question you ask yourself. When are you going to make some changes? What are you doing to live that fulfilled life you've always wanted to live? What are you doing to get closer to our creator? What are you doing to bring forth and manifest the gift that almighty God has given you? What are you doing to make this a better world with your gifts? What are you doing to help those who are in need?

If what you're doing feels good to the heart and soul, you are on the right track. If you're uneasy or not sure of what you're doing, rethink and reevaluate that activity.

Pay more attention to how you use your words. Many times we don't realize the effects our words have on our lives and others' lives. Speaking is a form of doing. It can and does have severe consequences if we're not careful in how we use our words. This goes along with the "How's My Thinking?" part of this material. After thinking, we must do something. Doing is a critical part of the process. Thinking, speaking, and doing are three levels of creation. We use them all the time, and sometimes we're unaware of how they truly affect our lives. We think, we speak, and we take action.

"The word became flesh." Here is my interpretation of that: Before God said the word, God thought. Then God said the word, and the word became flesh or matter. A word is the same as a thought, but only at a different frequency, vibration, or energy. Flesh or matter is the same as a word, but only at a different frequency, vibration, or energy. It's the same as water in different forms like steam, water, and ice. They're the same stuff, only at different frequencies. This is analogous to a gas, liquid, and solid. They are only at different frequencies. Thought becomes word, then flesh or matter, just as steam becomes water and then water becomes ice.

Be careful how you use your words. They may turn into a solid representation of an experience you don't desire.

Doing can sometimes be a challenge. We may know there's something we need to do, but we have difficulty getting started. I see it as overcoming the gravity of resistance and procrastination. Even while writing this information, I'm struggling with resistance and procrastination. I know I want to get it done, but I sometimes have to struggle with myself to continue writing. The thrust of my mind needs to be greater than the pull of resistance for me to escape complacency, just like a rocket has to overcome gravity to enter space.

Is there something you know you should be doing, but you just can't seem to get started? Make yourself start, and you'll see yourself becoming more and more motivated to complete the task. Life rewards action more than it does intention, insight, wisdom, or understanding. Come to know that it is time to begin translating our intention, insight, wisdom, and awareness into constructive, meaningful actions that will bring joy and fulfillment to ourselves and to the people we love.

Ask yourself, "How is my TEDDY today?"

# HOW ARE YOU?

The *Y* in TEDDY represents you. Are you happy? If not, do you want to be? Do you know if you're happy or not? Do you know what it takes to be happy?

After observing our lives when it comes to thinking, eating, exercising, drinking, and doing, it's time to take a look at the bigger picture.

The word "you" is small, but it carries the weight of your total physical, mental, and spiritual existence. You are greater than you can imagine. We have taught ourselves to believe that we are much less than who we really are. The world has given us a lot of false information about ourselves. We have forgotten who we are by design. We just don't know that we know, and at times we take ourselves for granted. You will find that prayer and meditation will cause you to have a deeper sence of who you are. You will also get answers that you didn't know through prayer and meditation. We don't know that we are love and light that's being temporarily covered by darkness.

This taking ourselves for granted will at some point come to an end after experiencing who we are *not*. After all, the mistakes we make in our lives, and the lessons learned from these mistakes, will bring us to a point of remembering who we are. We will have a better understanding of what we *don't* want in our lives.

Life has a tendency to wake us up to the things we have always known. At some point, we will become awakened. We don't choose what's going to wake us up. We have no idea what's going to show up to teach us the lessons we need to learn. We have no control over those special lessons we may encounter.

I have come to the point in my life when I monitor carefully what I'm thinking and feeling during unpleasant and pleasant events. I realize that my overall well-being determines how I handle my thinking and feelings. Maintaining a certain amount of joy during all situations is important to me at this stage of my life.

How are you now, after all you've experienced up to this point? Have you awakened to the now, or are you stuck in the dream of the past? Are you worried about the future?

What we call unpleasant experiences are going to happen no matter what we do or think, in spite of how we use our minds to attract our experiences, as I explained earlier. Have you noticed that our minds have a tendency to jump from one problem to the next? That's just the way the mind is. We think we're our thoughts. The reality is we're not our thoughts. We are the intelligence that is paying attention to the thoughts. We should avoid being caught up in the mind's erratic chatter and just observe it. We can learn how to still the mind. That is the only way we can free ourselves from ourselves. We are not the chatter that takes place in the mind. We are the observers. Who we are is in the silence that is the act of observation.

I have found that when I keep myself in the now or in the moment, I release myself from many concerns that really don't matter. All that we have is the now. All that we have is this moment. Tomorrow, or what we call the future, will only be an extension of the now. What we call yesterday is the now. All things occur sequentially and simultaneously in the now. Undesirable emotions live in thoughts of the so-called past or the so-called future. Love dwells in the light of the now or this moment. Fear dwells in dark memories of the so-called past and what we think may occur in the so-called future.

Have you ever noticed that we find ourselves worrying about things that turn out completely different from what we expected? Yet we worried ourselves sick over what we thought would happen. You notice that I used the word "sick." That's because worrying brings on all types of physical and emotional illnesses. Stress and worry are two of the main causes of illness in our country.

How are you at this moment, while you're reading this book? Forget about what's happening outside you for a moment. Focus on your thoughts and your awareness of your thoughts. Are you full of fear, anxiety, or frustration about any seemingly big or small thing? You can change all of that. We are on the path to self-realization. The bottom line is that we want to free ourselves from ourselves. We want to free ourselves from our ego and from whatever worldly things we're experiencing that are preventing us from having joy in our lives.

How are you doing in that regard? Is your TEDDY on track to bringing you the kind of life you want to experience? After you have read this material and thought about your life, are you still in old habits, worrying, eating poorly, not exercising, and not resting? Are you still drinking acidic water and other acidic beverages? Are you spending your time doing things that aren't bringing you joy and contentment?

If your answer to any of these questions is yes, start making changes to improve your life. Your solution to worry, despair, or whatever negative situation you find yourself in can be found when you ask the question "How is my TEDDY?" The answers will ultimately bring you clarity. Then you must act.

TEDDY will help you to manifest your desires, and it will bring you closer to God, as it has done for me and for others. But first you must make the changes that are necessary. You must apply yourself. The more changes you make, the easier it will get. By not making these changes, you may have to "bear" the burden of living an unbalanced, unhealthy and unfulfilled life. Being happy, healthy and close to God are all that really matter.

Be aware of yourself, and once more ask yourself, "How is my TEDDY today?"

# DEDICATION

This book is dedicated to my mother, Etheal Young, who passed away on November 25, 2012; my wife, Cristal; my sons, Kareem, Khalil, and Rashad Young; Kathy and Butch Rivers; Jimmy and Janie Rivers; Bishop and Mary Young; Merdyth Harley; Albertha Alford; Cleveland Young; Harold Young, who passed away January 12, 2015; and my entire extended family. I would also like to dedicate it to Tommy and Mary Bryant; David and Geraldine Harris; Jun and Cathy Afable; Russell Lyles; Ariana and Kelley Brockington and their new baby boy, Shakia; Joe Thomason; and all my friends and customers who have supported us here at Central Electronics for the past twenty-five years.

# ACKNOWLEDGMENTS

First of all, I would like to acknowledge Almighty God for giving me the wisdom and health to accomplish the writing of this little book.

I thank my wife, Cristal, for the loving support she has given to this family during our many years of marriage.

I thank my long-time and good friend, David, and his wife, Geraldine Harris, for reading my early draft and giving me honest feedback, suggestions, and encouragement to complete this project.

I want to thank Marie Mitchell for being the first person I shared TEDDY with. After explaining the acronym to her, she gave me her approval, told me I was on to something, and encouraged me to complete this book.

Thanks to Marita Golden for giving me some very important information on finalizing this book. Thanks to her husband, Joeseph Murray, for his support.

Made in the USA
Middletown, DE
09 June 2015